The Solar System

Robin Birch

The Sun

CHELSEA CLUBHOUSE
An Imprint of Chelsea House Publishers
A Haights Cross Communications Company
Philadelphia

This edition first published in 2004 in the United States of America by Chelsea Clubhouse, a division of Chelsea House Publishers and a subsidiary of Haights Cross Communications.

Chelsea House Publishers
1974 Sproul Road, Suite 400
Broomall, PA 19008-0914

The Chelsea House world wide web address is www.chelseahouse.com

Library of Congress Cataloging-in-Publication Data Applied for.
ISBN 0-7910-7934-1

First published in 2004 by
MACMILLAN EDUCATION AUSTRALIA PTY LTD
627 Chapel Street, South Yarra, Australia, 3141

Associated companies and representatives throughout the world.

Edited by Anna Fern
Text and cover design by Cristina Neri, Canary Design
Illustrations by Melissa Webb
Photo research by Legend Images

Printed in China

Acknowledgements
The author and publisher are grateful to the following for permission to reproduce copyright material:

Cover photograph of the Sun courtesy of Photodisc.

Michael Jensen/Auscape, p. 22; Tom Till/Auscape, p. 5 (bottom); Australian Picture Library/Corbis, p. 4; Wendy Carlos & Jay M. Pasachoff/SOHO, p. 11; Corbis Digital Stock, p. 23 (top); Digital Vision, pp. 5 (top), 6, 7, 13, 25; ESA/NASA/SOHO, p. 29; Calvin J. Hamilton, p. 9; Marie Lochman/Lochman Transparencies, p. 23 (bottom); NASA/MIX, p. 27 (bottom); Photodisc, pp. 12, 14, 15; Photolibrary.com/SPL, pp. 8, 10, 19, 21, 26, 27 (top), 28.

Background and border images, including view of the Sun, courtesy of Photodisc.

Please note
At the time of printing, the Internet addresses appearing in this book were correct. Owing to the dynamic nature of the Internet, however, we cannot guarantee that all these addresses will remain correct.

Contents

The Sun   4

The Sun Is a Star   6

On the Sun   10

Sun and Earth   16

Studying the Sun   26

Sun Fact Summary   30

Glossary   31

Index   32

Glossary words

When you see a word printed in bold, **like this**, you can look up its meaning in the glossary on page 31.

People have always seen the Sun in the sky. **Ancient** peoples worshipped the Sun, which brought light and warmth for their crops to grow.

The ancient Greeks worshipped the Sun god Helios. They believed that Helios drove the Sun across the sky in a horse-drawn chariot.

▲ This is the symbol for the Sun.

▶ Helios

Later, the ancient Romans adopted Helios as their Sun god and called him "Apollo." The ancient Chinese people's Sun god traveled across the sky in a chariot drawn by dragons. The ancient Egyptians had four Sun gods. The most important was Ra, the god of the midday Sun.

Until the 1500s, the Mayan, Incan, and Aztecan peoples of Central and South America all built temples for Sun worship. The temples lined up with the rising and setting Sun, which helped the people follow the seasons.

▲ The Sun

Ancient English people erected stone circles that helped them follow the Sun across the seasons. One example is Stonehenge, which was built between 3000 and 2000 B.C.

In ancient times, people used to believe that the Sun circled around Earth. It was only about 400 years ago that people understood that Earth circles around the Sun. Today, people study the Sun with **telescopes**, and send **space probes** to gather information about it.

▼ Stonehenge

5

The Sun Is a Star

The Sun is a star. It is a huge ball of very hot, glowing **gas**, like other stars.

Sun's Formation

The Sun formed in a huge cloud of hydrogen gas. The gas swirled around and formed a tight ball, and heated up. When the gas ball reached a temperature of 18 million degrees Fahrenheit (10 million degrees Celsius), nuclear fusion began inside it.

In nuclear fusion, hydrogen particles join together to make particles of the substance helium. When they do this, huge amounts of heat and light energy are given off.

When nuclear fusion began in the ball of gas, the ball became a star, the Sun. This happened about 4,600 million years ago.

The ancient Romans called the Sun "*Sol*." Today the official name for the Sun is "Solaris."

▶ This gas cloud has young stars in it.

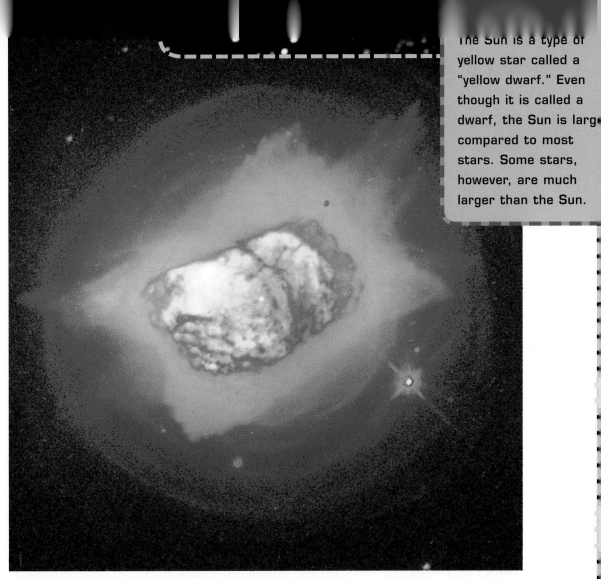

▲ This dying star is throwing off gas.

In about 5,000 million years from now, the Sun will run out of hydrogen gas. Then nuclear fusion in the **core** will stop, and a different type of nuclear fusion will spread into the outer layers. The Sun will expand and become a red color. It will then be what is called a "red giant" star. The Sun will probably be so large at this time that it will swallow up Earth.

The red giant Sun will eventually collapse. As it collapses, it will throw off gas. The Sun's core will become an object called a "white dwarf."

The Solar System

The solar system consists mainly of the Sun and nine planets, which **orbit** the Sun.

The Sun formed at the center of a huge cloud of gas. At the same time, many other bodies formed and were spread throughout the cloud. These other bodies became planets, **moons** of the planets, comets, and asteroids, which all orbit the Sun. The Sun and all the bodies which orbit it are called "the solar system." The Sun's **gravity** keeps the other objects circling around it.

The Sun lights up the other bodies, which mostly do not make their own light.

▼ The solar system

The Planets

There are nine planets orbiting the Sun. They are made of rock, ice, gas, and liquid. Mercury, Venus, Earth, and Mars are made of rock. Pluto is probably made of rock and ice. These are the smallest planets.

Jupiter, Saturn, Uranus, and Neptune are made mainly of gases and liquids. They are the largest planets. They are often called the gas giants, because they have no solid ground to land on.

Asteroids are rocks which orbit the Sun. There are millions of them. Comets are large balls of rock, ice, gas, and dust which orbit the Sun. They grow tails when they get close to the Sun.

Planet	Average distance from Sun	
Mercury	35,960,000 miles	(57,910,000 kilometers)
Venus	67,190,000 miles	(108,200,000 kilometers)
Earth	92,900,000 miles	(149,600,000 kilometers)
Mars	141,550,000 miles	(227,940,000 kilometers)
Jupiter	483,340,000 miles	(778,330,000 kilometers)
Saturn	887,660,000 miles	(1,429,400,000 kilometers)
Uranus	1,782,880,000 miles	(2,870,990,000 kilometers)
Neptune	2,796,000,000 miles	(4,504,000,000 kilometers)
Pluto	3,672,300,000 miles	(5,913,520,000 kilometers)

▲ The planets, from smallest to largest, are: Pluto, Mercury, Mars, Venus, Earth, Neptune, Uranus, Saturn, and Jupiter.

On the Sun

The huge, hot Sun is the closest star to Earth. It orbits the center of the **galaxy**, speeding through space at 137 miles (220 kilometers) every second.

Size and Structure

The Sun is 863,000 miles (1,390,000 kilometers) in **diameter**. It is about 109 times wider than Earth.

The center of the Sun, called the core, has a temperature of 27 million degrees Fahrenheit (15 million degrees Celsius). The core is where nuclear fusion takes place. In the nuclear fusion, hydrogen is converted into helium. Energy is released from this process, which makes the Sun's heat and light.

Outside the Sun's core is the radiative zone and then the convective zone. The energy released in the core takes one million years to pass through these layers and reach the surface.

Convective zone

Photosphere

Radiative zone

Core

▶ Parts of the Sun

▲ The Sun's corona shows up during a total solar eclipse.

The outside surface of the Sun is called the photosphere. Around the photosphere is a thin layer of gas known as the chromosphere. Outside the chromosphere is another layer of gas called the corona. The corona extends a long way out from the Sun.

The Sun is about 75 percent hydrogen and 25 percent helium. However, the hydrogen is gradually being converted to helium. Over time, there will be less and less hydrogen, and more and more helium.

Photosphere

The surface layer of the Sun, called the photosphere, is about 300 miles (500 kilometers) thick. It has a mottled appearance, like boiling water. The temperature of the photosphere is 9,900 degrees Fahrenheit (5,500 degrees Celsius). The energy produced in the Sun's core is released from the photosphere as heat and light.

The photosphere **rotates** at different speeds in different places. At the Sun's **equator**, the photosphere rotates once every 25.4 days. At the **poles**, the photosphere takes up to 36 days to rotate once. The Sun can rotate at different speeds because it is made of gas.

"Photosphere" means "sphere of light."

▼ The surface of the Sun has a mottled appearance.

Chromosphere

The chromosphere is a layer of hot gas which is just above the photosphere. It is about 1,600 miles (2,500 kilometers) thick. The lower part of the chromosphere is cooler, then its temperature rises to about 18,000 degrees Fahrenheit (10,000 degrees Celsius) towards the top.

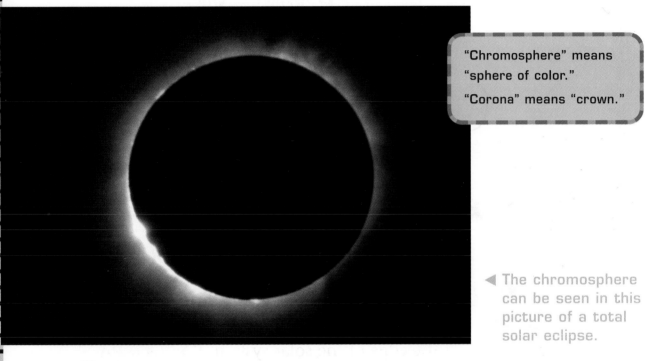

"Chromosphere" means "sphere of color."

"Corona" means "crown."

◀ The chromosphere can be seen in this picture of a total solar eclipse.

Corona

The Sun's corona is an area of very thin gas which extends millions of miles from the Sun. It reaches temperatures of millions of degrees and is heated by **magnetic** energy from the Sun. It cannot be heated by the Sun's surface, as the surface is much cooler. The corona can be seen in pictures of a total solar eclipse. The corona becomes the solar wind, as it passes through the solar system.

Sunspots

Sunspots are spots on the Sun's photosphere. They appear dark because they are cooler than the gas around them. Their temperature is about 6,300 degrees Fahrenheit (3,500 degrees Celsius). Sunspots are usually found in groups. Their number builds up over a period of 11 years, then drops. The size of sunspots can range from a few hundred miles across to larger than Earth.

Solar Flares

Solar flares are eruptions of gas and energy from parts of the photosphere that have sunspots. There are more solar flares when there are more sunspots.

Solar Prominences

Solar prominences are huge solar flares which leap long distances from the Sun.

▲ A solar prominence

▼ An aurora on Earth

The solar wind blows comet tails away from the Sun.

Solar Wind

The solar wind is the name given to the part of the Sun's corona which stretches to the edge of the solar system. It is a stream of **charged** particles which spreads out from the Sun in all directions. It usually takes about a week for the particles to travel from the Sun to Earth.

When the charged particles in the solar wind reach Earth, some get trapped in Earth's **magnetic field**. Sometimes they fall towards the ground near the North and South poles. They make curtains of light in the sky, called "auroras," or the northern or southern lights. When the solar wind blows more strongly, it can affect electricity supplies and radio communications.

15

Sun and Earth

The Sun's energy supports life on Earth. The Sun is also the main force behind Earth's seasons and weather.

Day and Night

Earth rotates on its **axis** once every 24 hours. Because of this, we see the Sun rise in the east, pass across the sky, and set in the west. The Sun appears to move, but it is really Earth that is moving.

From most of the Northern **Hemisphere**, the Sun is seen passing through the southern sky. From most of the Southern Hemisphere, the Sun is seen passing through the northern sky.

Never look straight at the Sun, even with sunglasses. It will burn your eyes if you look at it.

Sun

Axis

Day

Night

▲ Where the Sun shines onto Earth, it is daytime.

▲ Seasons on Earth

Seasons

Earth **revolves** around the Sun in one year. Earth's axis is tilted, which causes seasons on Earth.

When the Northern Hemisphere is tilted towards the Sun, it has summer. The Sun rises north of east, and sets north of west. When the Northern Hemisphere is tilted away from the Sun, it has winter. The Sun rises south of east, and sets south of west.

When the Southern Hemisphere is tilted towards the Sun, it has summer. The Sun rises south of east, and sets south of west. When the Southern Hemisphere is tilted away from the Sun, it has winter. The Sun rises north of east, and sets north of west.

Sunshine in the Seasons

In summer, the Sun reaches high in the sky at midday. When the Sun shines onto the ground, the heat rays do not pass through as much air as they do in winter. The air in the **atmosphere** cools the Sun's heat rays down. As the rays of the summer Sun pass through less air than they do in winter, the summer Sun is hotter than in winter.

In winter, the midday Sun is lower in the sky than in summer. The Sun's heat rays pass through more air than they do in summer. This cools them down, making the Sun cooler in winter than in summer.

▼ The Sun's rays in winter   ▼ The Sun's rays in summer

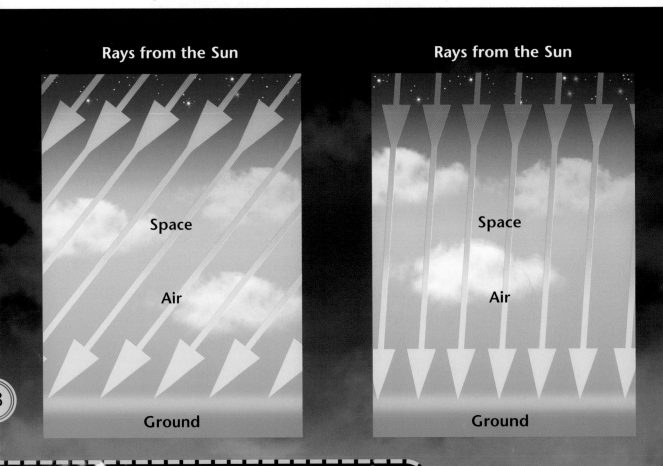

Rays from the Sun   Rays from the Sun

Space   Space

Air   Air

Ground   Ground

	Northern Hemisphere	Southern Hemisphere
Spring equinox	about March 21	about September 22
Summer solstice	about June 21	about December 22
Fall equinox	about September 22	about March 21
Winter solstice	about December 22	about June 21

▲ Close to the North Pole and the South Pole, the longest summer day lasts for days or weeks.

Solstices and Equinoxes

The longest day of the year is called the summer solstice. This day is the beginning of summer. The shortest day of the year is called the winter solstice. It is the beginning of winter. The equinoxes are times of year when day and night are equal in length. The fall equinox is the beginning of fall and the spring equinox is the beginning of spring.

The North and South poles of Earth have one long summer daytime, where the Sun does not set for six months. In winter, the night lasts for six months. In places near the poles, summer days are very long, and winter nights are very long.

Rays from the Sun

The Sun **radiates** different kinds of rays. The rays we can see are called visible light. The other rays are gamma rays, X rays, ultraviolet rays, infrared rays, and radio waves.

Earth's atmosphere stops dangerous gamma rays, X rays, and ultraviolet rays from reaching the ground. Visible-light rays light up Earth, and infrared rays heat Earth.

▼ Earth's atmosphere stops some of the Sun's rays.

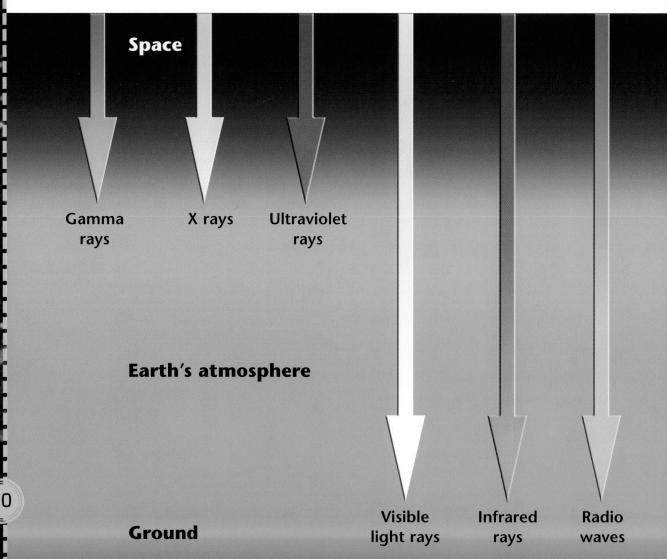

Space

Gamma rays

X rays

Ultraviolet rays

Earth's atmosphere

Ground

Visible light rays

Infrared rays

Radio waves

▲ The Sun's spectrum, seen through a spectrometer

We see the Sun's spectrum when there is a rainbow. The sunlight is broken up by the water drops in the sky.

The Color of Sunlight

Sunlight is a white color. When it shines though a prism, such as a piece of cut glass, the white light breaks up into rainbow colors, called a spectrum.

An instrument for collecting a spectrum is called a spectrometer. A spectrum made from sunlight by a spectrometer looks like a piece of a rainbow with thin black lines across it. The lines are caused by different substances on the outside of the Sun, such as iron and sodium. **Astronomers** have discovered a lot of detailed information about the Sun by studying its spectrum.

Sun Energy

Sunlight is used to make electricity. Solar cells collect sun energy and make electricity for many different uses, from operating toys, to powering cars and homes.

Heat from the Sun is collected to heat water for use in homes and swimming pools. This is known as solar heating.

Heat from the Sun drives the weather on Earth. The Sun heats up water so that it **evaporates**. The water collects in clouds, then falls as rain. The Sun also heats up air, which produces winds.

▼ Solar cells on the roof of a solar-powered vehicle

▲ Animals eat plants grown in sunlight.

Energy for Living Things

The Sun gives living things the energy they need. Plants use sunlight to make their food in a process called "photosynthesis." Without sunlight, plants cannot make their food. Animals eat plants to get their energy. In this way, animals also rely on sunlight for their energy.

Plants and animals need water to live. The Sun is warm enough to melt ice, so that there is water, but not so hot that the water dries up. The Sun provides warmth for living things. It is not too hot and not too cold.

▶ Reptiles are cold-blooded, and need heat from the Sun to warm up.

Solar Eclipses

Once a month, the Moon passes between Earth and the Sun. Usually the Sun and the Moon do not line up exactly, so the Moon does not block out the Sun's light. However, sometimes the Moon does line up exactly with the Sun, and does block the Sun's light. This is called a solar eclipse, or an eclipse of the Sun.

The Sun and the Moon are almost exactly the same size in the sky. This is because the Sun is 400 times wider than the Moon, but it is 400 times further away. When the Moon covers the Sun exactly, the sky goes dark. This is called a total eclipse. If the Moon only partly covers the Sun, it is called a partial eclipse, and the sky stays bright.

▼ During a solar eclipse, the Moon's shadow darkens part of Earth.

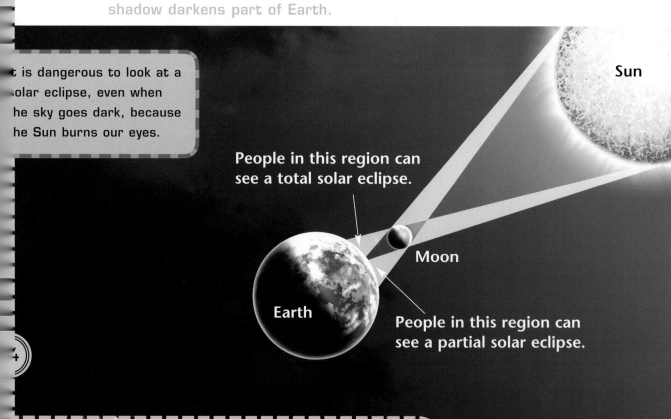

It is dangerous to look at a solar eclipse, even when the sky goes dark, because the Sun burns our eyes.

People in this region can see a total solar eclipse.

Sun

Moon

Earth

People in this region can see a partial solar eclipse.

▼ A total solar eclipse

When the sky goes dark during a total solar eclipse, the stars shine, the temperature goes down, and birds settle down on the trees.

Total Eclipses

A total solar eclipse can last for up to 8 minutes, but usually lasts for only about 2 minutes. The Sun's corona shows up as glowing light around the Moon. The pink chromosphere also shows up around the edge of the Moon, along with pink solar prominences leaping from the Sun's surface.

When there is a total solar eclipse, it only occurs along a long but narrow path on Earth. Many people travel long distances to observe a total solar eclipse. Partial solar eclipses occur over a much wider area.

Studying the Sun

People have been studying the Sun since ancient times. Today, space probes and solar telescopes help us to learn about the Sun.

The Sun was first studied by the ancient Greeks and Romans, who mostly believed that Earth was the center of the **universe**, and the Sun circled around it. A Greek astronomer, Aristarchus, who was born in 310 B.C., realized the Sun was much bigger than the Moon, and farther away. He also thought the planets circled around the Sun. Other astronomers at the time did not believe him.

In 1543, Nicolaus Copernicus again suggested that Earth circled the Sun. He was not believed until telescopes gave new information, about 100 years later. Today, we know that nine planets orbit the Sun.

▲ Nicolaus Copernicus

Nicolaus Copernicus was a Polish astronomer, born in 1473. He was a church official and a doctor.

Solar Telescopes

Astronomers use special telescopes, called solar telescopes, to study the Sun. Other telescopes would burn our eyes very quickly if we looked at the Sun through them. Solar telescopes have a mirror at the top which turns to face the Sun. The mirror reflects the Sun's light down a tube, where it is shone onto a screen, where it can be looked at and photographed. This is a safe way of observing the Sun.

▼ This picture was taken by *Skylab* astronauts in 1973.

▲ A solar telescope

One way of taking good pictures of the Sun is to photograph it from space. *Skylab* was a space station which orbited Earth in 1973 and 1974. It had a crew of three **astronauts** who took more than 150,000 pictures of the Sun, using solar telescopes.

▼ *Ulysses*

Space Probes

Many space probes have studied the Sun. They detect X rays and ultraviolet rays coming from the Sun, as well as light rays.

The *Ulysses* probe was launched in 1990. Its aim is to observe the north and south poles of the Sun, and to detect what may be in space high above them. *Ulysses* discovered holes in the corona above the poles.

The space probe *SOHO* (short for *"Solar and Heliospheric Observatory"*) was launched in 1995. Its aim is to help astronomers work out the structure inside the Sun, and to watch how the Sun's surface rises and falls. Astronomers also want to use *SOHO* to study the Sun's corona and the solar wind, by collecting ultraviolet light.

Questions about the Sun

There is still a lot to learn about the Sun, and astronomers will continue to send space probes to study it. One day, astronomers hope to find out the answers to questions such as these:

- Why is the Sun's corona so much hotter than the photosphere? It would seem impossible that the corona could get hotter higher up.
- What is the exact cause of sunspots?
- What would be found in space above and below the poles of the Sun? Earth revolves around the Sun's equator, and we really only know about our part of space.

▲ *SOHO*

Sun Fact Summary

Diameter	863,000 miles (1,390,000 kilometers)
Mass	333,000 times Earth's mass
Density	1.41 times the density of water
Gravity	27.9 times Earth's gravity
Temperature (at surface)	9,900 degrees Fahrenheit (5,500 degrees Celsius)
Rotation on axis	25.4 Earth days (at equator)
Revolution around galaxy	220 million years
Planets	9

Web Sites

www.astro.uva.nl/demo/sun/kaft.htm
The Sun

www.nineplanets.org/
The nine planets—a tour of the solar system

www.enchantedlearning.com
Enchanted Learning web site—click on "Astronomy"

stardate.org
Stargazing with the University of Texas McDonald Observatory

Glossary

ancient lived thousands of years ago

astronauts people who travel in space

astronomers people who study stars, planets, and other bodies in space

atmosphere a layer of gas around a large body in space

axis an imaginary line through the middle of an object, from top to bottom

charged carrying electric energy

core the inside, or middle part

density a measure of how heavy something is for its size

diameter the distance across

equator an imaginary line around the middle of a globe

evaporates changes from a liquid into a gas

galaxy a huge group of many millions of stars (the solar system is in the Milky Way galaxy)

gas a substance in which the particles are far apart, so they are not solid or liquid

gravity a force which pulls one body towards another body

hemisphere half of a globe

magnetic has force which affects magnetic particles

magnetic field an area which affects magnetic particles

mass a measure of how much substance is in something

moons natural bodies which circle around planets

orbit *noun* the path a body takes when it moves around another body *verb* to travel on a path around another body in space

poles the top and bottom of a globe

radiates gives off something

revolves travels around another body

rotates spins

space probes spacecraft which do not carry people

telescopes instruments for making far away objects look bigger and more detailed

universe all of space

Index

A

Aristarchus 26
asteroids 8, 9
astronauts 27, 31
astronomers 21, 26–9,
    31
atmosphere (Earth) 18,
    20, 31
auroras 15

C

chromosphere 10, 11,
    14, 25
comets 8, 9, 15
convective zone 10
Copernicus, Nicolaus 26
core (Sun) 7, 10, 12, 31
corona 10, 11, 14–15,
    25, 28, 29

D

day 16, 19

E

Earth 7, 15, 16–19,
    22–3, 24–5, 26, 29
eclipses 11, 14, 24–5
energy (solar) 6, 10, 12,
    13, 14, 22–3
equator (Sun) 12, 29, 31
equinoxes 19

F

formation (Sun) 6, 8

G

gamma rays 20
gas giants 9
gravity 8, 30, 31

H

helium 6, 10, 11
hydrogen 6, 7, 10, 11

I

infrared rays 20

L

life 23

M

magnetic field (Earth)
    15, 31
Moon (Earth's) 24–5, 26
moons 8, 31

N

night 16, 19
nuclear fusion 6–7, 10

O

observing the Sun 5, 21,
    25, 26–8
orbit (Sun) 10, 31

P

photosphere 10, 11,
    12–13, 29
photosynthesis 23
planets 8–9, 26, 30
plants 4, 23
poles (Earth) 15, 19, 31
poles (Sun) 12, 28, 29,
    31

R

radiative zone 10
radio waves 20
rainbows 21
rays 18, 20
red giants 7
rotation (Sun) 12, 30, 31

S

seasons 5, 16, 17–19
size (Sun) 10, 12, 14, 30
Skylab 27
SOHO 28, 29
solar flares 13
solar prominences 13, 25
solar system 8–9, 26
solar telescopes 5, 26, 27
solar wind 14–15, 28
solstices 19
space probes 5, 26, 28,
    29, 31
spectrometers 21
spectrums 21
star death 7
stars 6–7
structure (Sun) 10–15,
    28
Sun worship 4–5
sunspots 12–13, 29

T

temperature (Sun) 6, 10,
    12, 13, 14, 29, 30

U

ultraviolet rays 20, 28
Ulysses 28

V

visible light 20–21, 28

W

water 23
white dwarves 7
winds 22

X

X rays 20, 28

Y

yellow dwarves 7